LEARNING ABOUT THE EARTH

Tundra

by Colleen Sexton

BELLWETHER MEDIA • MINNEAPOLIS, MN

Note to Librarians, Teachers, and Parents:

Blastoff! Readers are carefully developed by literacy experts and combine standards-based content with developmentally appropriate text.

Level 1 provides the most support through repetition of high-frequency words, light text, predictable sentence patterns, and strong visual support.

Level 2 offers early readers a bit more challenge through varied simple sentences, increased text load, and less repetition of high-frequency words.

Level 3 advances early-fluent readers toward fluency through increased text and concept load, less reliance on visuals, longer sentences, and more literary language.

Level 4 builds reading stamina by providing more text per page, increased use of punctuation, greater variation in sentence patterns, and increasingly challenging vocabulary.

Level 5 encourages children to move from "learning to read" to "reading to learn" by providing even more text, varied writing styles, and less familiar topics.

Whichever book is right for your reader, Blastoff! Readers are the perfect books to build confidence and encourage a love of reading that will last a lifetime!

This edition first published in 2011 by Bellwether Media, Inc.

Library of Congress Cataloging-in-Publication Data
Sexton, Colleen A., 1967–
 Tundra / by Colleen Sexton.
   p. cm. — (Blastoff! readers. Learning about the earth)
 Includes bibliographical references and index.
 Summary: "Simple text and full-color photographs introduce beginning readers to the characteristics and geographical locations of tundra. Developed by literacy experts for students in kindergarten through third grade"—Provided by publisher.
 ISBN 978-0-531-26038-8 (paperback : alk. paper)
 1. Tundras–Juvenile literature. 2. Tundra ecology–Juvenile literature. I. Title.
 GB571.S49 2009
 551.45'3–dc22   2008013327

Printed in the United States of America.   010111   1185

Contents

Tundra is cold, flat land.
Trees do not usually
grow on tundra.

Tundra is very dry.
Fewer than 20 inches
(50 centimeters) of
rain and snow fall
each year.

Arctic tundra lies north of the **Arctic Circle**. This area is at the top of the earth close to the **North Pole**.

Winters are long and cold in the Arctic. There is little sunlight.

Tundra stays frozen most of the year. Ice and snow cover the ground.

The tundra changes when summer and sunlight come to the Arctic.

The top layer of
tundra thaws.
Beneath that layer
is a layer that does
not thaw. It is called
permafrost.

Permafrost is earth that stays frozen year-round. In some places, permafrost is 4,500 feet (1,220 meters) thick.

Water from melted ice and snow cannot soak into the permafrost. The water stays in the tundra's top layer.

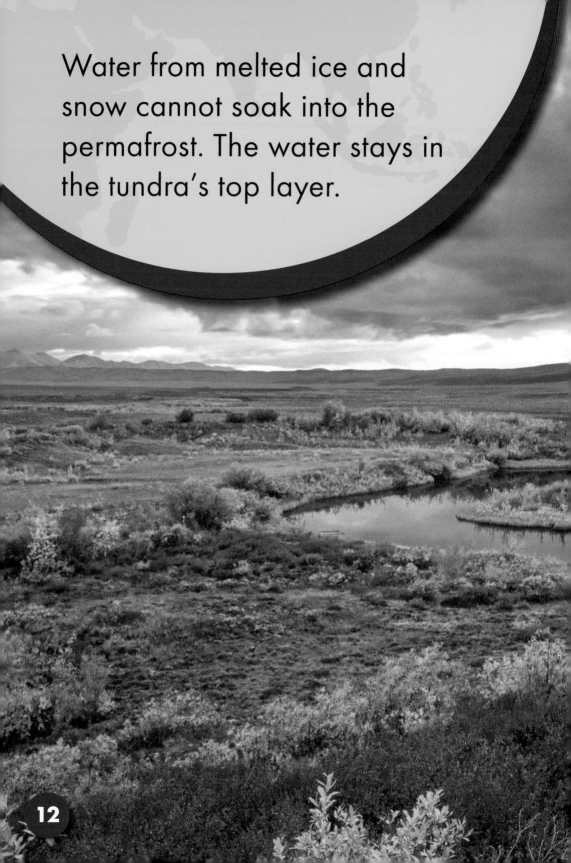

The ground in the top layer becomes soft and wet. Water fills lakes and ponds.

Tundra is mostly flat. However, the freezing and thawing of water change the land.

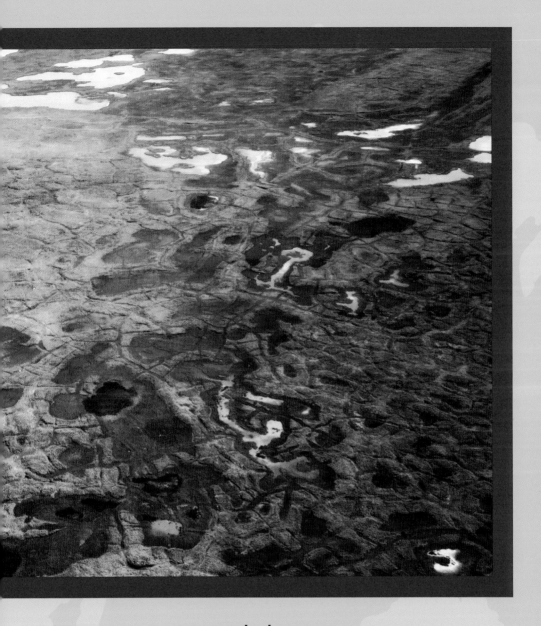

Freezing and thawing create cracks, bumps, and valleys. Cone-shaped hills called **pingos** rise from the land.

Patterns form on the tundra when it thaws. Dirt and pebbles make striped patterns on hills. Cracks in flat land form groups of multi-sided shapes called **polygons**.

Small **shrubs** and plants grow in the tundra's top layer during summer. Trees cannot grow on most tundra. They cannot take root in the tundra's permafrost.

Buttercups, poppies, and other small flowers bloom. **Lichens** spread in patches of green, orange, white, and yellow.

Some animals live on the tundra year-round. Musk oxen have thick fur coats to protect them from the cold. Lemmings stay warm in underground tunnels.

In winter, Arctic foxes turn white. They blend in with the snow when they hunt.

Some animals are visitors. Caribou come to graze on summer plants. Ducks, geese, arctic terns, and other birds nest in the tundra in summer. They **migrate** south when winter returns to the tundra.

Glossary

Arctic Circle—an imaginary line around the top of the earth; the area north of this line is called the Arctic.

lichen—a living thing that grows on rocks and trees; a lichen is made up of a kind of algae and a fungus that grow together.

migrate—to move from one place to another; some animals migrate with the seasons; they move south to warmer places when the weather gets cold.

North Pole—the northernmost point on the earth

permafrost—a layer of earth that is always frozen; permafrost is covered by a top layer of soil 10 to 35 inches (25 to 90 centimeters) thick.

pingo—a cone-shaped hill that has ice on the inside and soil on the outside

polygon—on the tundra, this is a shape bordered on each side by a crack in the land; many polygons together make a pattern on the tundra.

shrub—a plant with woody branches that is smaller than a tree; shrubs grow low to the ground on the tundra.

To Learn More

AT THE LIBRARY

Marsico, Katie. *A Home on the Tundra*. New York: Children's Press, 2007.

Stone, Lynn M. *Tundra*. Vero Beach, Fla.: Rourke, 2004.

Wadsworth, Ginger. *Tundra Discoveries*. Watertown, Mass.: Charlesbridge, 1999.

ON THE WEB

Learning more about tundra is as easy as 1, 2, 3.

1. Go to www.factsurfer.com

2. Enter "tundra" into search box.

3. Click the "Surf" button and you will see a list of related web sites.

With factsurfer.com, finding more information is just a click away.

Index

The images in this book are reproduced through the courtesy of: John E. Marriott / age fotostock, front cover, pp. 9, 12-13; George Burba, pp. 4, 14-15; Andre Gallant / Getty Images, pp. 6-7; Bryan & Cherry Alexander Photography / Alamy, pp. 8, 16; Panoramic Images / Getty Images, p. 11; Getty Images, p. 17; Dale Wilson / Masterfile, p. 18; Thomas Kitchin & Victoria Hurst / Getty Images, p. 19; Yva Momatiuk / John Eastcott / Getty Images, p. 20.